The Astronomers

Also by Edgar Bowers

The Form of Loss

The
Astronomers

EDGAR BOWERS

ALAN SWALLOW
DENVER

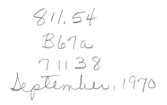

© 1965 by Edgar Bowers

Library of Congress Catalog Number: 65-17011

This book is for my mother and her sisters

SECOND PRINTING

Contents

I

II

Some of the poems in this volume have appeared in the following periodicals and are reprinted with the permission of their editors: *Poetry, New Statesman, Chrysalis, Spectrum, Virginia Quarterly, New York Times, Paris Review, Sewanee Review.*

I

The Astronomers of Mont Blanc

Who are you there that, from your icy tower,
Explore the colder distances, the far
Escape of your whole universe to night;
That watch the moon's blue craters, shadowy crust,
And blunted mountains mildly drift and glare,
Ballooned in ghostly earnest on your sight;
Who are you, and what hope persuades your trust?

It is your hope that you will know the end
And compass of our ignorant restraint
There in lost time, where what was done is done
Forever as a havoc overhead.
Aging, you search to master in the faint
Persistent fortune which you gaze upon
The perfect order trusted to the dead.

Adam's Song to Heaven

You shall be as gods, knowing good and evil

O depth sufficient to desire,
Ghostly abyss wherein perfection hides,
    Purest effect and cause, you are
The mirror and the image love provides.

All else is waste, though you reveal
Lightly upon your luminous bent shore
    Color, shape, odor, weight, and voice,
Bright mocking hints that were not there before,

And all your progeny time holds
In timeless birth and death. But, when, for bliss,
    Loneliness would possess its like,
Mine is the visage yours leans down to kiss.

Beautiful you are, fair deceit!
Knowledge is joy where your unseeing eyes
    Shine with the tears that I have wept
To be the sum of all your thoughts devise.

Flawless you are, unlimited
By other than yourself, yet suffer pain
    Of the nostalgias I have felt
For love beyond the end your eyes contain;

    Then, solitary, drift, inert,
Through the abyss where you would have me go
    And, lost to your desire at last,
Ravish the waste for what you cannot know.

    What are you then! Delirium
Receives the image I despair to keep,
    And knowledge in your somber depth
Embraces your perfection and your sleep.

An Afternoon at the Beach

I'll go among the dead to see my friend.
The place I leave is beautiful: the sea
Repeats the winds' far swell in its long sound,
And, there beside it, houses solemnly
Shine with the modest courage of the land,
While swimmers try the verge of what they see.

I cannot go, although I should pretend
Some final self whose phantom eye could see
Him who because he is not cannot change.
And yet the thought of going makes the sea,
The land, the swimmers, and myself seem strange,
Almost as strange as they will someday be.

Of an Etching

Toward me, seated, young, spent by war, bend two,
Lover, mother, perhaps, future and past,
Memory of peace, worn tranquillity.
But I, seated on a tomb, ride the swift
Invisible wave: young, weary, estranged,
Turn toward you, gazing over my shoulder,
Forgetting. Forgetting armor's embrace,
Riding the tomb, lonely, suffering myself,
I, present forever, forever turn
Toward you, stranger, for whom I stay the same
Young man, both self and mortuary urn.

To Death

If I am but the unmysterious sum
Of each event which all the past has sealed
        And I repeat,
You are the mark of that delirium
By which desire for limit is revealed,
        And for defeat
To which I understand I, too, must come.

If I can only be as I have been
And yet through timeless time and spaceless space
        Vary by chance,
You are the trust which my pretended pain
And hope and purpose form here in the grace
        Of circumstance,
The grace I cannot prove but would sustain.

Dear mercy, with your old ambiguous smile,
Meaningless life contrives your sacrifice.
        Though all event
Ignore your magnitude a little while,
Your claim is real, and must at last suffice
        All who dissent,
Our comfort, and the limit of our guile.

To the Contemporary Muse

Honesty, little slut, must you insist
On hearing every dirty word I know
And all my worst affairs? Are impotence,
Insanity, and lying what you lust for?
Your hands are cold, feeling me in the dark.

In a darkness

I watch no comfort bent across the grass
Which was my shadow. Here, alone, I pass
Bereft of him whose trust I took on trust.
And, bound by neither lust nor thought of lust,
By neither warmth nor cold, stand so alone,
So exiled to some future monotone,
That should my hand grope upward to my face,
All it could touch might seem a little space.
Even its dim report might cease, somewhere
Between the ends of darkness and of air.

In the Last Circle

You spoke all evening hatred and contempt,
The ethical distorted to a fury
Of self-deception, malice, and conceit,
Yourself the judge, the lawyer, and the jury.
I listened, but, instead of proof, I heard,
As if the truth were merely what you knew,
Wrath cry aloud its wish and its despair
That all would be and must be false to you.

You are the irresponsible and damned,
Alone in final cold athwart your prey.
Your passion eats his brain. Compulsively,
The crime which is your reason eats away
Compassion, as they both have eaten you,
Till what you are is merely what you do.

The Mirror

Father, I loved you as a child, and still,
When trouble bruises him whom I retrace
Back to the time I cannot know, I fill,
By my desire, the possible with grace,
And wait your coming. Then I see my face,
Breathed by some other presence on the chill
Illumination of this mortal glass,
Gleam from the dark to struggle in your will.

In that fixed place, around me, others move,
Vivid with long conclusion, who, once dead,
Quickened the little moment I could prove;
And, though I seem to live, there, at my head,
As if the thought translating all I see,
He stands, who was my future, claiming me.

After Leconte de Lisle

Under the dense sycamore, she sleeps,
Virginal, in a garden white and dry.
An azure butterfly
Has escaped the shade to hover at her lips.

Long the sun polishes the white sky.
While, steeped in silence, through the sleeping grapes,
The future wakes, she sleeps,
Dreams, her chaste mouth smiling as the blue light sips.

Spirit kiss possessing her rapt lips
Awakens in her cool, deep, leafy sleep
Love without human shape,
Young desire aroused to grave activity.

Revery swims! Soundless the dark sleep
It swims through. The white garden of the sky
Is soundless. Her pale lips
Smile, gravely she sleeps; nothing moves, still he sips.

Awake, awake! Empty gardens sleep;
Dreaming the deep immaculate sky, they sleep,
Fade, vanish — not a shape
But fades, uncertain in that pure intensity.

Dream no more! Awake, lest, in your sleep,
Desire, oblivious, vanish where the deep,
Silent, immaculate sky
Will keep you sleeping, dreaming forever of sleep.

An Answer

Most difficult and dear, here on my bed,
Your sorrow, more than your old fabled love,
Moves in me what remains for it to move
Of love and pity; and, uncomforted,
And frank as the assent it would inspire,
Tempts me to trust, once more, my own desire.

Though I have labored and lie down to rest,
I cannot sleep, fearing that you might be
Nailed there awake and waiting on the tree.
But, if I doubt my doubt as self-possessed,
I cannot help but wonder whether shame
Or scorn or hurt murmurs your dreadful name.

I try by words to imitate your word,
Though I know that my speech, even if true,
Names only what is not the same as you;
And, as I must, I know my death conferred
On every flesh and see, revealed to sense,
The enormity of perfect difference.

I am my first and last, but, though, too late,
Dumb, blind, and certain, change will mend this dim
Unfaithful likeness of its antonym,
I cannot comfort you, if you should wait,
Passionate in your logical intent,
For me to know how else I dare assent.

A Song for Rising

My life is mine to have well or to lose.
I struggle to conceive, not who I am,
But, in the constant end that I must choose,
The being that permits me to its sum.

Even by that attempt I must profane
The certain no pretense of mine can change,
From which each hopeful lie departs in vain.
I am the brief departure lies derange.

So here I am at last, and you are there,
The same as you have always been, the true,
The final and the necessary care.
All that I am and hope to be is you.

But why you are or why I am or why
I think to ask I will no longer guess.
The manifest dilemma that was I
Confronted you between its nothingness.

The Dream

I dreamed last night I dreamed, and in that sleep
You called me from the stair, as if the dead
Command each fragile sleeper to awake
And free them from their darkened wandering.
I knew that you would come into the room.
I waited for the sudden tug and slant
Upon the edge of my vague spectral bed.
I woke, looked at my watch, and sucked my breath.
There, in my stead, still waiting and still true,
Lay him who dreamed me still and, maybe, you.

The Centaur Overheard

Once I lived with my brothers, images
Of what we know best and can best become.
What I might be I learned to tell in eyes
Which loved me. Voices formed my name,

Taught me its sound, released me from its dread.
Now they are all gone. When I prance, the sound
From dark caves where my hooves disturb the dead
Orders no other promise. Underground,

Streams urge their careless motion into air.
I stand by springs to drink. Their brimming poise
Repeats the selfish hope of who comes there.
But I do not look, move, or make a noise.

II

Autumn Shade

1.

The autumn shade is thin. Grey leaves lie faint
Where they will lie, and, where the thick green was,
Light stands up, like a presence, to the sky.
The trees seem merely shadows of its age.
From off the hill, I hear the logging crew,
The furious and indifferent saw, the slow
Response of heavy pine; and I recall
That goddesses have died when their trees died.
Often in summer, drinking from the spring,
I sensed in its cool breath and in its voice
A living form, darker than any shade
And without feature, passionate, yet chill
With lust to fix in ice the buoyant rim —
Ancient of days, the mother of us all.
Now, toward his destined passion there, the strong,
Vivid young man, reluctant, may return
From suffering in his own experience
To lie down in the darkness. In this time,
I stay in doors. I do my work. I sleep.
Each morning, when I wake, I assent to wake.
The shadow of my fist moves on this page,
Though, even now, in the wood, beneath a bank,
Coiled in the leaves and cooling rocks, the snake
Does as it must, and sinks into the cold.

2.

Nights grow colder. The Hunter and the Bear
Follow their tranquil course outside my window.
I feel the gentian waiting in the wood,
Blossoms waxy and blue, and blue-green stems
Of the amaryllis waiting in the garden.
I know, as though I waited what they wait,
The cold that fastens ice about the root,
A heavenly form, the same in all its changes,
Inimitable, terrible, and still,
And beautiful as frost. Fire warms my room.
Its light declares my books and pictures. Gently,
A dead soprano sings Mozart and Bach.
I drink bourbon, then go to bed, and sleep
In the Promethean heat of summer's essence.

3.

Awakened by some fear, I watch the sky.
Compelled as though by purposes they know,
The stars, in their blue distance, still affirm
The bond of heaven and earth, the ancient way.
This old assurance haunts small creatures, dazed
In icy mud, though cold may freeze them there
And leave them as they are all summer long.
I cannot sleep. Passion and consequence,
The brutal given, and all I have desired
Evade me, and the lucid majesty
That warmed the dull barbarian to life.
So I lie here, left with self-consciousness,
Enemy whom I love but whom his change
And his forgetfulness again compel,
Impassioned, toward my lost indifference,
Faithful, but to an absence. Who shares my bed?
Who lies beside me, certain of his waking,
Led sleeping, by his own dream, to the day?

4.

If I ask you, angel, will you come and lead
This ache to speech, or carry me, like a child,
To riot? Ever young, you come of age
Remote, a pledge of distances, this pang
I notice at dusk, watching you subside
From tree-tops and from fields. Mysterious self,
Image of the fabulous alien,
Even in sleep you summon me, even there,
When, under his native tree, Odysseus hears
His own incredible past and future, whispered
By wisdom, but by wisdom in disguise.

5.

Thinking of a bravura deed, a place
Sacred to a divinity, an old
Verse that seems new, I postulate a man
Mastered by his own image of himself.
Who is it says, *I am*? Sensuous angel,
Vessel of nerve and blood, the impoverished heir
Of an awareness other than his own?
Not these, but one to come? For there he is,
In a steel helmet, raging, fearing his death,
Carrying bread and water to a quiet,
Placing ten sounds together in one sound:
Confirming his election, or merely still,
Sleeping, or in a colloquy with the sun.

6.

Snow and then rain. The roads are wet. A car
Slips and strains in the mire, and I remember
Driving in France: weapons-carriers and jeeps;
Our clothes and bodies stiffened by mud; our minds
Diverted from fear. We labor. Overhead,
A plane, Berlin or Frankfurt, now New York.
The car pulls clear. My neighbor smiles. He is old.
Was this our wisdom, simply, in a chance,
In danger, to be mastered by a task,
Like groping round a chair, through a door, to bed?

7.

A dormant season, and, under the dripping tree,
Not sovereign, ordering nothing, letting the past
Do with me as it will, I savor place
And weather, air and sun. Though Hercules
Confronts his nature in his deed, repeats
His purposes, and is his will, intact,
Magnificent, and memorable, I try
The simplest forms of our old poverty.
I seek no end appointed in my absence
Beyond the silence I already share.

8.

I drive home with the books that I will read.
The streets are harsh with traffic. Where I once
Played as a boy amid old stands of pine,
Row after row of houses. Lined by the new
Debris of wealth and power, the broken road.
Then miles of red clay bank and frugal ground.
At last, in the minor hills, my father's place,
Where I can find my way as in a thought —
Gardens, the trees we planted, all we share.
A Cherokee trail runs north to summer hunting.
I see it, when I look up from the page.

9.

In nameless warmth, sun light in every corner,
Bending my body over my glowing book,
I share the room. Is it with a voice or touch
Or look, as of an absence, learned by love,
Now, merely mine? Annunciation, specter
Of the worn out, lost, or broken, telling what future,
What vivid loss to come, you change the room
And him who reads here. Restless, he will stir,
Look round, and see the room renewed, and line,
Color, and shape as, in desire, they are,
Not shadows but substantial light, explicit,
Bright as glass, inexhaustible, and true.

10.

My shadow moves, until, at noon, I stand
Within its seal, as in the finished past.
But in the place where effect and cause are joined,
In the warmth or cold of my remembering,
Of love, of partial freedom, the time to be
Trembles and glitters again in windy light.
For nothing is disposed. The slow soft wind
Tilting the blood-root keeps its gentle edge.
The intimate cry, both sinister and tender,
Once heard, is heard confined in its reserve.
My image of myself, apart, informed
By many deaths, resists me, and I stay
Almost as I have been, intact, aware,
Alive, though proud and cautious, even afraid.